Call #	Client	Company	Date	Time	Notes

Call #					

Call #	Client	Company	Date	Time	Notes

Call #	Client	Company	Date	Time	Notes

Call #	Client	Company	Date	Time	Notes

Call #	Client	Company	Date	Time	Notes

Call #	Client	Company	Date	Time	Notes

Call #	Client	Company	Date	Time	Notes

Call #	Client	Company	Date	Time	Notes

Call #	Client	Company	Date	Time	Notes

Call #	Client	Company	Date	Time	Notes

Call #	Client	Company	Date	Time	Notes

Call #	Client	Company	Date	Time	Notes

Call #	Client	Company	Date	Time	Notes

Call #	Client	Company	Date	Time	Notes

Call #	Client	Company	Date	Time	Notes

Call #	Client	Company	Date	Time	Notes

Call #	Client	Company	Date	Time	Notes

Call #	Client	Company	Date	Time	Notes

Call #	Client	Company	Date	Time	Notes

Call #	Client	Company	Date	Time	Notes

Call #	Client	Company	Date	Time	Notes

Call #	Client	Company	Date	Time	Notes

Call #	Client	Company	Date	Time	Notes

Call #	Client	Company	Date	Time	Notes

Call #	Client	Company	Date	Time	Notes

Call #	Client	Company	Date	Time	Notes

Call #	Client	Company	Date	Time	Notes

Call #	Client	Company	Date	Time	Notes

Call #	Client	Company	Date	Time	Notes

Call #	Client	Company	Date	Time	Notes

Call #	Client	Company	Date	Time	Notes

Call #	Client	Company	Date	Time	Notes

Call #	Client	Company	Date	Time	Notes

Call #	Client	Company	Date	Time	Notes

Call #	Client	Company	Date	Time	Notes

Call #	Client	Company	Date	Time	Notes

Call #	Client	Company	Date	Time	Notes

Call #	Client	Company	Date	Time	Notes

Call #	Client	Company	Date	Time	Notes

Call #	Client	Company	Date	Time	Notes

Call #	Client	Company	Date	Time	Notes

Call #	Client	Company	Date	Time	Notes

Call #	Client	Company	Date	Time	Notes

Call #	Client	Company	Date	Time	Notes

Call #	Client	Company	Date	Time	Notes

Call #	Client	Company	Date	Time	Notes

Call #	Client	Company	Date	Time	Notes

Call #	Client	Company	Date	Time	Notes

Call #	Client	Company	Date	Time	Notes

Call #	Client	Company	Date	Time	Notes

Call #	Client	Company	Date	Time	Notes

Call #	Client	Company	Date	Time	Notes

Call #	Client	Company	Date	Time	Notes

Call #	Client	Company	Date	Time	Notes

Call #	Client	Company	Date	Time	Notes

Call #	Client	Company	Date	Time	Notes

Call #	Client	Company	Date	Time	Notes

Call #	Client	Company	Date	Time	Notes

Call #	Client	Company	Date	Time	Notes

Call #	Client	Company	Date	Time	Notes

Call #	Client	Company	Date	Time	Notes

Call #	Client	Company	Date	Time	Notes

Call #	Client	Company	Date	Time	Notes

Call #	Client	Company	Date	Time	Notes

Call #	Client	Company	Date	Time	Notes

Call #	Client	Company	Date	Time	Notes

Call #	Client	Company	Date	Time	Notes

Call #	Client	Company	Date	Time	Notes

Call #	Client	Company	Date	Time	Notes

Call #	Client	Company	Date	Time	Notes

Call #	Client	Company	Date	Time	Notes

Call #	Client	Company	Date	Time	Notes

Call #	Client	Company	Date	Time	Notes

Call #	Client	Company	Date	Time	Notes

Call #	Client	Company	Date	Time	Notes

Call #	Client	Company	Date	Time	Notes

Call #	Client	Company	Date	Time	Notes

Call #	Client	Company	Date	Time	Notes

Call #	Client	Company	Date	Time	Notes

Call #	Client	Company	Date	Time	Notes

Call #	Client	Company	Date	Time	Notes

Call #	Client	Company	Date	Time	Notes

Call #	Client	Company	Date	Time	Notes

Call #	Client	Company	Date	Time	Notes

Call #	Client	Company	Date	Time	Notes

Call #	Client	Company	Date	Time	Notes

Call #	Client	Company	Date	Time	Notes

Call #	Client	Company	Date	Time	Notes

Call #	Client	Company	Date	Time	Notes

Call #	Client	Company	Date	Time	Notes

Call #	Client	Company	Date	Time	Notes

Call #	Client	Company	Date	Time	Notes

Call #	Client	Company	Date	Time	Notes

Call #	Client	Company	Date	Time	Notes

Call #	Client	Company	Date	Time	Notes

Call #	Client	Company	Date	Time	Notes

Call #	Client	Company	Date	Time	Notes

Call #	Client	Company	Date	Time	Notes

Call #	Client	Company	Date	Time	Notes

Call #	Client	Company	Date	Time	Notes

Call #	Client	Company	Date	Time	Notes

Call #	Client	Company	Date	Time	Notes

Call #	Client	Company	Date	Time	Notes

Call #	Client	Company	Date	Time	Notes

www.ingramcontent.com/pod-product-compliance
Lightning Source LLC
Chambersburg PA
CBHW070100210526
45170CB00012B/663